THAT'S MY JAM!

R & B MUSIC

BY NATHAN SOMMER

eureka!

EUREKA!, AN IMPRINT OF BELLWETHER MEDIA BY FLUTTERBEE

Eureka! books turn real stories into unforgettable experiences. Clear, direct language and sharp, captivating imagery make it easy to follow your curiosity, one fascinating fact at a time. Your Eureka! moment awaits!

This edition first published in 2027 by Bellwether Media, Inc.

For information regarding permission, write to Bellwether Media, Inc., Attention: Permissions Department, 3500 American Blvd W, Suite 150, Bloomington, MN 55431.

Names: Sommer, Nathan author
Title: R & B music / Nathan Sommer.
Description: Eureka. | Minneapolis : Bellwether Media, Inc, 2027. | Series: That's my jam! | Includes index. | Audience: Ages 9-13 | Audience: Grades 7-9 | Summary: ""Engaging images accompany information on R&B music. The text level and subject matter are intended for students in grades 5 through 9"-Provided by publisher" -- Provided by publisher.
Identifiers: LCCN 2026013876 (print) | LCCN 2026013877 (ebook) | ISBN 9798898801274 (library binding) | ISBN 9798898802516 (ebook)
Subjects: LCSH: Rhythm and blues music--History and criticism
Classification: LCC ML3521 2027 .S56 (print) | LCC ML3521 2027 (ebook) | DDC 781.644--dc23/eng/20260318

LC record available at https://lccn.loc.gov/2026013876
LC ebook record available at https://lccn.loc.gov/2026013877

Editor: Elizabeth Neuenfeldt Designer: Josh Brink

Printed in the United States of America, North Mankato, MN.

TABLE OF CONTENTS

WHAT IS R & B?

R & B stands for rhythm and blues. This genre pairs strong, soulful vocals with smooth, bass-heavy beats. Its artists often use keyboards and drum machines. Modern R & B includes elements of pop and hip-hop. Its songs have emotional themes. Many focus on love and heartbreak. Others address the struggles of life.

BEYONCÉ

BEHIND THE NAME

The phrase "rhythm and blues" has existed since the 1940s. It was first written by *Billboard* writer Jerry Wexler. It described a genre that had existed since the 1920s.

Soul and funk are popular R & B subgenres. New jack swing is popular too. The biggest R & B stars today include Beyoncé and Bruno Mars.

THE HISTORY OF R & B

R & B started in the 1940s. It is rooted in Black music. It grew from gospel, jazz, and blues. It replaced swing music from earlier times. Early R & B shared qualities with rock and roll. The electric guitar was a key instrument at the time. Early hitmakers included B.B. King and Fats Domino.

MOTOWN RECORDS

Detroit, Michigan, is one of the cities where modern R & B was born. Berry Gordy Jr. founded Motown Records there in 1959. It helped launch artists such as the Supremes and Stevie Wonder.

B.B. KING

FATS DOMINO

R & B was soulful in the 1960s. Smoother, church-inspired production took over. Marvin Gaye and Aretha Franklin were superstars.

R & B grew in the 1970s. Funk and disco took over. Artists began using electronic instruments. This created more danceable music. New jack swing began in the 1980s. It blended R & B with hip-hop. This made Janet Jackson and Bobby Brown household names.

THE GOLDEN AGE

Many call the 1990s the golden age of R & B. It had many successful R & B artists. Subgenres such as neo-soul also took off.

Mariah Carey and Mary J. Blige were stars in the 1990s. They often collaborated with rappers. Soulful ballads and slow jams were also popular. Joss Stone and Amy Winehouse gained popularity in the 2000s. Today's R & B stars mix R & B, pop, and hip-hop. Bruno Mars and the Weeknd top charts.

R & B TIMELINE

1940s
The phrase "rhythm and blues" is first used

1949
R & B as a genre is added to *Billboard* charts

1959
Berry Gordy Jr. founds Motown Records, soon launching the careers of many R & B superstars

1964
Robert Moog invents the modern synthesizer, an instrument that produces many R & B beats

1967
Aretha Franklin's landmark R & B hit "Respect" is released

ARETHA FRANKLIN

BERRY GORDY JR.

ROBERT MOOG

MARVIN GAYE

1969

The Songwriters Hall of Fame is founded, soon becoming a top honor for R & B artists

1971

Marvin Gaye's iconic *What's Going On* comes out, leaving a lasting mark on R & B

1980s

New jack swing becomes a popular new subgenre blending R & B with hip-hop beats

TEDDY RILEY

1990

The golden age of R & B begins, making stars out of many new artists

WHITNEY HOUSTON

BEYONCÉ

2025

Beyoncé wins her 35th Grammy, the most of any artist in history

INSTRUMENTS

BASS GUITARS

Bass guitars were first made in the 1930s by Paul Tutmarc. The first modern bass guitars were made in the 1950s. This instrument gives R & B songs low, rhythmic sounds.

DRUM MACHINES

Leon Theremin and Henry Cowell created the first drum machine. They invented it in the 1930s. Unlike live drums, its sounds can be mixed and edited. It gives many R & B songs their rhythm.

ANCIENT INSTRUMENTS

Musical keyboards have been used for over 2,000 years. The earliest one was called the hydraulis. It was a series of levers. It was used in ancient Greece.

SYNTHESIZERS

Synthesizers create sounds that can be edited digitally. They have produced many of modern R & B's warm, layered beats. The instrument was invented by Robert Moog in 1964.

CORY HENRY

AWARDS AND HONORS

BET AWARDS

The BET Awards honor Black artists. They were first held in 2001. Top categories include Album of the Year and Best Female R & B/Pop Artist. Beyoncé has the most wins overall.

A LIFETIME ACHIEVEMENT

Artists must write for more than 20 years before being added to the Songwriters Hall of Fame. It honors a lifetime of songwriting success.

GRAMMY AWARDS

The Grammys began in 1959. They honor music's top artists. Top R & B awards include Best R & B Song and Best R & B Album.

SONGWRITERS HALL OF FAME

The Songwriters Hall of Fame was created in 1969. It honors music's greatest storytellers. R & B artists added to it include Mariah Carey and Marvin Gaye.

TYPES OF R & B

SOUL

Date Started: late 1950s

Traits:
- blends gospel with R & B
- powerful rhythms
- emotional vocals and storytelling

Song: "Midnight Train to Georgia" by Gladys Knight & the Pips

FUNK

Date Started: late 1960s

Traits:
- danceable and high-energy beats
- heavy guitar use
- improvised vocals and melodies

Song: "Brick House" by the Commodores

MARIAH CAREY

GLORIA GAYNOR

SLOW JAMS

Date Started: early 1980s

Traits

- slow, relaxed pace
- smooth and soulful melodies
- often focus on love and romance

Song: "Babydoll" by Mariah Carey

DISCO

Date Started: late 1960s

Traits:

- fast-paced electronic production
- layered use of horn and string instruments
- sing-along choruses

Song: "I Will Survive" by Gloria Gaynor

NEO-SOUL

Date Started: 1990s

Traits:
- ◊ blends modern R & B with soul
- ◊ frequent use of samples
- ◊ vocals that mix singing and speaking

Song: "Ex-Factor" by Lauryn Hill

POP R & B

Date Started: 1980s

Traits:
- ◊ catchy, radio-friendly melodies
- ◊ beats often made with synthesizers

Song: "Cry Me a River" by Justin Timberlake

ALTERNATIVE R & B

Date Started: around the 2000s

Traits:

- combines R & B with other genres
- experimental production
- often has emotional themes

Song: "Saturn" by SZA

SZA

NEW JACK SWING

Date Started: mid 1980s

Traits:

- hip-hop- and jazz-inspired beats
- heavy use of drum machines
- harmonized vocals

Song: "Any Time, Any Place" by Janet Jackson

JANET JACKSON

R & B PROFILES
ARETHA FRANKLIN

Aretha Franklin is the Queen of Soul. She is one of music's most influential artists.

CHILD GOSPEL STAR

Franklin's parents were gospel singers. As a teen, she performed with her father around the country. Her first album came out in 1956.

Birthday:
March 25, 1942

Death:
August 16, 2018

Hometown:
Memphis, Tennessee

Types of Music:
soul, gospel

First Hit Song:
"I Never Loved a Man (The Way I Love You)" (1967)

TIMELINE

1956
Franklin's debut album is released

1967
"Respect" is released, becoming the most famous song of Franklin's career

1972
Amazing Grace is released, later becoming history's best-selling gospel album

A LITTLE RESPECT

Franklin's 1967 song "Respect" was an anthem for civil rights. *Rolling Stone* named it the best song of all time in 2024. Franklin's 1967 song "Chain of Fools" topped *Billboard*'s R & B chart. Her 1972 album *Amazing Grace* is history's best-selling gospel album.

HALL OF FAME HISTORY

Franklin won 18 Grammys. In 1987, she became the first woman added to the Rock & Roll Hall of Fame.

A PRESIDENTIAL HONOR

Franklin was awarded the Presidential Medal of Freedom in 2005. It honors people whose work has helped change art and other fields.

HIT RELEASES

- ***I Never Loved a Man the Way I Love You*** **(1967)**
- ***Lady Soul*** **(1968)**
- ***Aretha Now*** **(1968)**
- ***Amazing Grace*** **(1972)**
- ***Who's Zoomin' Who?*** **(1985)**

1987
Franklin becomes the first woman added to the Rock & Roll Hall of Fame

2005
Franklin is awarded the Presidential Medal of Freedom

MARVIN GAYE

Marvin Gaye is nicknamed the Prince of Motown. His work advocated for social change.

FROM STREET CORNERS TO SUCCESS

Gaye sang doo-wop music on street corners as a teen. He joined the group the Moonglows in 1959. His major 1960s hits included "Ain't No Mountain High Enough" and "I Heard It Through the Grapevine."

Birthday:
April 2, 1939

Death:
April 1, 1984

Hometown:
Washington, D.C.

Types of Music:
doo-wop, soul, funk

First Hit Song:
"Stubborn Kind of Fellow" (1962)

SELF-PRODUCED PIONEER

Gaye wrote and produced the album *What's Going On* in 1971. Its songs were against war and racism. He won his first two Grammys in 1983.

HIT RELEASES

What's Going On
(1971)

I Want You
(1976)

Here, My Dear
(1978)

Midnight Love
(1982)

BREAKING THE NORM

Gaye produced his own music. This was uncommon during his time. His work showed R & B could cover topics beyond love.

TIMELINE

1959
Gaye joins the doo-wop group the Moonglows

1961
Gaye signs with Motown Records, kicking off his solo career

1968
"I Heard It Through the Grapevine" becomes Gaye's first *Billboard* Hot 100 chart-topper

1971
***What's Going On* comes out, later becoming one of R & B's most famous albums**

1983
Gaye wins his first two Grammys

DIANA ROSS

Diana Ross is a music and film icon. She brought global attention to R & B.

A SUPREME TALENT

Ross joined the group that became the Supremes in 1959. Their hits "Baby Love" and "You Can't Hurry Love" ruled 1960s R & B. She made her solo debut in 1970.

THE SUPREMES

ENTERTAINER OF THE CENTURY

Ross earned an Oscar nomination for 1972's *Lady Sings the Blues*. She was named *Billboard*'s Female Entertainer of the Century in 1976. Her 1980 album *Diana* included the hits "Upside Down" and "I'm Coming Out."

TIMELINE

1959
The group that became the Supremes is formed

1970
Ross makes her solo debut

1973
Ross receives an Oscar nomination for her role in *Lady Sings the Blues*

Birthday:
March 26, 1944

Hometown:
Detroit, Michigan

Types of Music
soul, disco, pop R & B

First Hit Song:
"Where Did Our Love Go" (1964)

OPENING NEW DOORS

Ross received the Lifetime Achievement Award at the 2012 Grammys. Her career helped create new opportunities for Black female artists.

A HISTORIC GROUP

The Supremes are one of the most successful groups in music history. They scored 12 chart-toppers on the *Billboard* Hot 100.

HIT RELEASES

- ***Diana Ross*** (1970)
- ***Touch Me in the Morning*** (1973)
- ***The Boss*** (1979)
- ***Diana*** (1980)
- ***Why Do Fools Fall in Love*** (1981)

1976
Ross is named *Billboard*'s Female Entertainer of the Century

2012
Ross receives the Grammy Lifetime Achievement Award

STEVIE WONDER

Stevie Wonder is a musical genius. He used electronic instruments to change R & B's sound.

CHILD WONDER

Wonder became blind shortly after birth. He played the piano, drums, and harmonica growing up. He topped the *Billboard* Hot 100 with "Fingertips (Part 2)" at age 13.

Birthday:
May 13, 1950

Hometown:
Saginaw, Michigan

Types of Music:
soul, funk, pop R & B

First Hit Song:
"Fingertips (Part 2)" (1963)

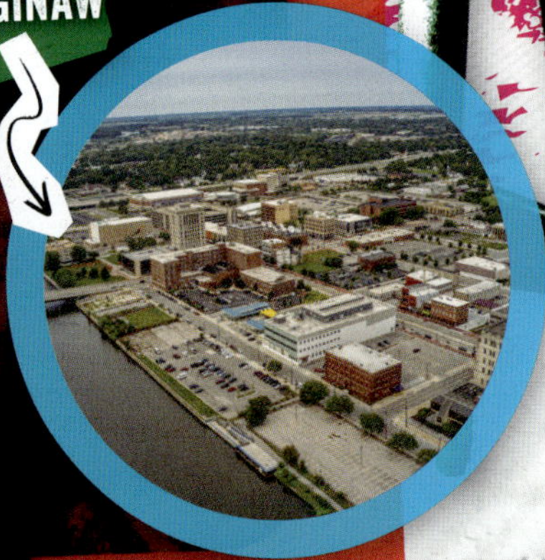

HIT RELEASES

Talking Book (1972)

Innervisions (1973)

Fulfillingness' First Finale (1974)

Songs in the Key of Life (1976)

Hotter than July (1980)

A HOT STREAK

Wonder's 1972 album *Talking Book* pioneered synthesizer use in R & B. It also included the mega hit "Superstition." Wonder won five Grammys in 1973. It was one of three times he won the Grammy for Album of the Year.

GRAMMY ICON

Wonder has won 25 Grammys. He has 10 *Billboard* Hot 100 chart-toppers. He was added to the Songwriters Hall of Fame in 1983.

TIMELINE

1961
Wonder signs with Motown Records at age 11

1963
Wonder earns his first of 10 *Billboard* Hot 100 chart-toppers

1972
Talking Book is released, pioneering synthesizer use in R & B

1973
Wonder wins five Grammys in one night

1983
Wonder is added to the Songwriters Hall of Fame

JANET JACKSON

Janet Jackson ruled R & B for decades. Her artistic independence blazed new trails for female artists.

A FAMOUS FAMILY

Jackson began performing with the Jackson 5 at age seven. They were her brothers. Her debut album came out in 1982.

HIT RELEASES

Control
(1986)

Rhythm Nation 1814
(1989)

janet.
(1993)

The Velvet Rope
(1997)

All for You
(2001)

TAKING CONTROL

Jackson left her family's management in 1985. Her 1989 album *Rhythm Nation 1814* scored seven top five hits. Her 1997 album *The Velvet Rope* pioneered alternative R & B. In 2001, "All for You" became Jackson's 10th Hot 100 chart-topper.

TIMELINE

1982
Jackson's debut album is released

1985
Jackson takes control of her career by leaving her family's management

1989
The *Rhythm Nation 1814* album scores seven top five singles

FROM MUSIC TO FILM

Jackson has also starred in many movies. Her famous roles include *Poetic Justice* and *For Colored Girls.*

A NEW GENERATION

Jackson has sold over 180 million records. Her work helped create a new generation of R & B.

Birthday:
May 16, 1966

Hometown:
Gary, Indiana

Types of Music:
new jack swing, pop R & B, alternative R & B

First Hit Song:
"Young Love" (1982)

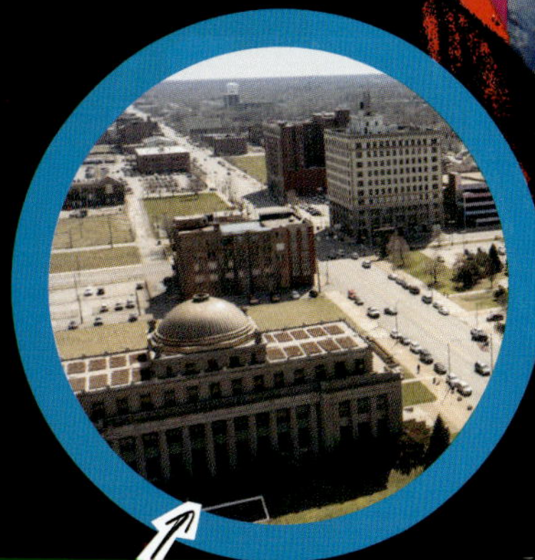

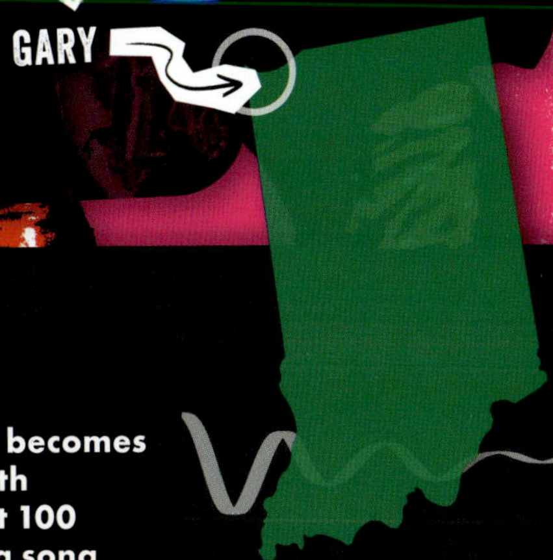

1997
The Velvet Rope is released, pioneering alternative R & B

2001
"All for You" becomes Jackson's 10th *Billboard* Hot 100 chart-topping song

WHITNEY HOUSTON

Whitney Houston is nicknamed the Voice. Her powerful vocals raised the bar for R & B artists.

TEEN MODEL

Houston performed with church choirs growing up. She modeled for *Cosmopolitan* and *Seventeen* magazines as a teen.

Birthday:
August 9, 1963

Death:
February 11, 2012

Hometown:
Newark, New Jersey

Types of Music:
pop R & B, soul

First Hit Song:
"You Give Good Love" (1985)

UNBELIEVABLE SUCCESS

Houston's first two albums scored seven Hot 100 chart-toppers. Her major hits included "How Will I Know" and "I Wanna Dance With Somebody." Houston starred in 1992's *The Bodyguard*. She won three Grammys for its iconic soundtrack. It is one of music's best-selling albums.

A MOST-AWARDED ARTIST

Houston is the most-awarded female artist of all time. She has won more than 400 awards.

HIT RELEASES

Whitney Houston
(1985)

Whitney
(1987)

I'm Your Baby Tonight
(1990)

The Bodyguard
(1992)

My Love Is Your Love
(1998)

TIMELINE

1985
Houston's first album is released

1988
"Where Do Broken Hearts Go" becomes Houston's seventh of 11 *Billboard* chart-toppers

1992
Houston stars in *The Bodyguard*, with its soundtrack later becoming one of history's best-selling albums

1994
Houston wins three Grammys in one night, including Album of the Year

2020
Houston is added to the Rock & Roll Hall of Fame

MARIAH CAREY

Mariah Carey is one of music's greatest songwriters. Her famous vocal range is five octaves.

A RECORD DEBUT

Carey's 1990 debut album scored four Hot 100 chart-topping songs. It later earned her two Grammys.

HIT RELEASES

Music Box **(1993)**

Daydream **(1995)**

Butterfly **(1997)**

Rainbow **(1999)**

The Emancipation of Mimi **(2005)**

QUEEN OF CHRISTMAS

Carey's song "All I Want for Christmas Is You" is Spotify's most-streamed Christmas song. Her holiday concerts draw large crowds each year.

TIMELINE

1990
Carey's first album is released, earning four *Billboard* Hot 100 chart-toppers

1991
Carey wins her first two Grammys, including Best New Artist

1999
"Heartbreaker" hits number one, giving Carey a chart-topping hit every year of the 1990s

R & B-RAP PIONEER

Carey topped the Hot 100 every year of the 1990s. Hits such as "Fantasy" and "Heartbreaker" pioneered the R & B-rap subgenre. Carey's 2005 album *The Emancipation of Mimi* won three Grammys. "We Belong Together" topped the Hot 100 chart for 14 weeks.

BILLBOARD ICON

Carey is the first artist to top the Hot 100 in four decades. Her 19 number one hits are the most of any solo artist.

Birthday:
March 27, 1969

Hometown:
Huntington, New York

Types of Music:
pop R & B, R & B-rap, slow jams

First Hit Song:
"Vision of Love" (1990)

2005
"We Belong Together" tops the Hot 100 for 14 weeks

2020
Carey becomes the first artist to top the Hot 100 in four different decades

USHER

Usher is a world-class performer. He mixes soulful vocals with high-energy dance moves.

TEEN IDOL

Usher was discovered on the talent show *Star Search*. He released his first album at age 15. His album *My Way* earned him *Billboard*'s 1998 Artist of the Year.

TOP-SELLING SUPERSTAR

Usher's 2004 album *Confessions* sold over 20 million copies. Its hits "Yeah!" and "My Boo" each won Grammys. In 2010, "OMG" became his ninth Hot 100 number one. He headlined 2024's Super Bowl Halftime Show.

Birthday:
October 14, 1978

Hometown:
Dallas, Texas

Types of Music:
pop R & B, R & B-rap

First Hit Song:
"Think of You" (1994)

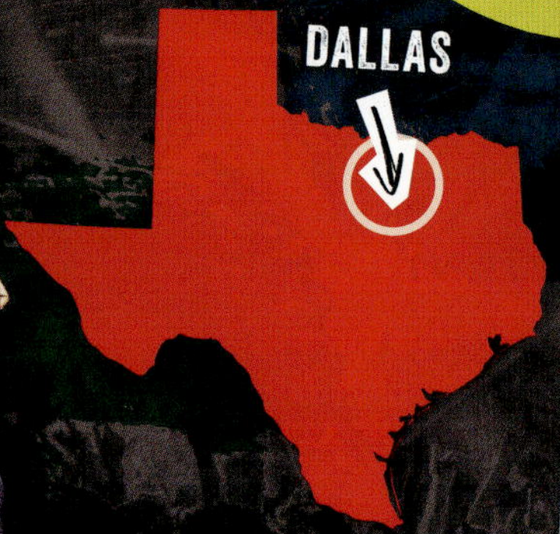

USHER

BLENDING GENRES

Usher has won eight Grammys. His blend of R & B with pop and hip-hop has left a lasting mark on the genre.

HIT RELEASES

- *My Way* (1997)
- *8701* (2001)
- *Confessions* (2004)
- *Here I Stand* (2008)
- *Raymond v. Raymond* (2010)

TIMELINE

1994
Usher's first album comes out

1998
Usher wins *Billboard*'s Artist of the Year

2004
The *Confessions* album is released, later selling over 20 million copies worldwide

2010
"OMG" becomes Usher's ninth Hot 100 number one hit

2024
Usher headlines the Super Bowl Halftime Show

BEYONCÉ

Beyoncé is one of music's most recognized names. Her boundary-pushing artistry has set new musical standards.

HIT RELEASES

- ***B'Day*** **(2006)**
- ***I Am... Sasha Fierce*** **(2008)**
- ***BEYONCÉ*** **(2013)**
- ***Lemonade*** **(2016)**
- ***Renaissance*** **(2022)**

DESTINY'S CHILD

Beyoncé joined Destiny's Child at age nine. They became one of history's best-selling girl groups. Her solo 2003 debut *Dangerously In Love* won five Grammys.

TIMELINE

1990
Beyoncé joins Destiny's Child, one of history's best-selling girl groups

2003
Beyoncé's debut album *Dangerously In Love* is released, later winning five Grammys

2008
"Single Ladies (Put A Ring On It)" is released, becoming one of the biggest hits of Beyoncé's career

SETTING NEW STANDARDS

Beyoncé's hits "Irreplaceable" and "Single Ladies (Put A Ring On It)" topped charts worldwide. Her visual albums *BEYONCÉ* and *Lemonade* changed how artists put out music. Beyoncé covers many genres. In 2022, *Renaissance* explored electronic music. In 2024, *COWBOY CARTER* featured country music.

A GRAMMY RECORD

Beyoncé won her 35th Grammy in 2025. She has the most Grammy wins and nominations of any artist in history.

Birthday:
September 4, 1981

Hometown:
Houston, Texas

Types of Music:
R & B, pop R & B, electronic, country

First Hit Song:
"Crazy In Love" (2003)

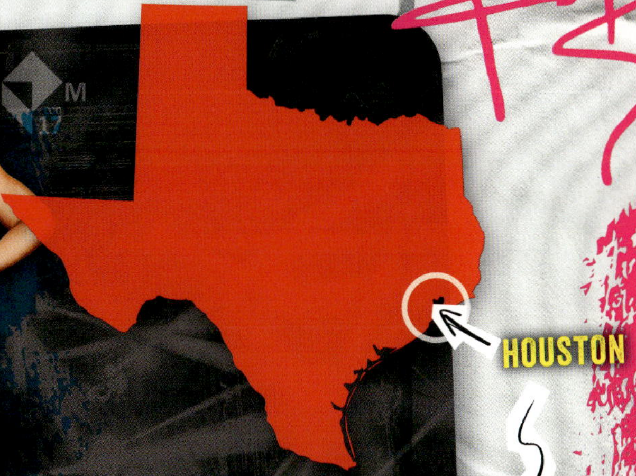

2013
The groundbreaking visual album *BEYONCÉ* comes out

2025
Beyoncé wins her record-breaking 35th Grammy

RIHANNA

Rihanna is a global superstar. She is also a billionaire businesswoman. Her music ruled 2000s and 2010s R & B.

CARIBBEAN BEGINNINGS

Rihanna grew up in Barbados. She won a high school talent show by performing a Mariah Carey song. Jay-Z later discovered her talent. Her first hit "Pon de Replay" came out in 2005.

HIT AFTER HIT

Rihanna's 2007 album *Good Girl Gone Bad* included the hit "Umbrella." Her 2016 album *Anti* highlighted alternative R & B sounds. Its song "Work" became her 14th Hot 100 chart-topper.

Birthday:
February 20, 1988

Hometown:
St. Michael, Barbados

Types of Music:
pop R & B,
alternative R & B

First Hit Song:
"Pon de Replay"
(2005)

HIT RELEASES

- ***Good Girl Gone Bad*** **(2007)**
- ***Loud*** **(2010)**
- ***Talk That Talk*** **(2011)**
- ***Unapologetic*** **(2012)**
- ***Anti*** **(2016)**

DIGITAL SUPERSTAR

Rihanna has won nine Grammys. She is the top-selling digital artist of all time.

BUSINESS HISTORY

Rihanna created the skincare company Fenty Beauty in 2017. She created the clothing brand Savage X Fenty in 2018. The brands made her the first Black woman with two billion-dollar companies.

TIMELINE

2005
"Pon de Replay" is released, hitting number two on the Hot 100

2008
Rihanna wins her first Grammy for Best Rap/Sung Collaboration for "Umbrella" with Jay-Z

2016
"Work" becomes Rihanna's 14th Hot 100 chart-topping hit

2018
"LOYALTY" with Kendrick Lamar earns Rihanna her ninth Grammy win

2025
Rihanna becomes the first Black woman with two billion-dollar companies

BRUNO MARS

Bruno Mars is one of the century's biggest hitmakers. He is known for his retro sound and flashy showmanship.

A YOUNG INSTRUMENTALIST

Mars played guitar, bass, piano, and percussion growing up. He wrote for other artists before his 2010 debut. The album included "Just the Way You Are" and "Grenade."

Birthday:
October 8, 1985

Hometown:
Honolulu, Hawai'i

Types of Music:
pop R & B, soul, funk

First Hit Song:
"Nothin' on You" featuring B.o.B. (2009)

STREAMING LEGEND

Mars's 2016 album *24K Magic* was inspired by 1990s R & B. It won Grammys for best song, record, and album. His 2024 song "Die With a Smile" was the fastest ever to reach one billion Spotify streams.

● POPULAR WINNER

Mars has sold 120 million records. As of 2026, he has won 16 Grammys.

HIT RELEASES

Doo-Wops & Hooligans (2010)

Unorthodox Jukebox (2012)

24K Magic (2016)

An Evening with Silk Sonic (2021)

TIMELINE

May 2010
"Nothin' on You" tops the Hot 100 chart

October 2010
Mars's debut album *Doo Wops & Hooligans* is released

2014
Mars becomes the youngest solo headliner of the Super Bowl Halftime Show

2018
24K Magic wins six Grammys

2024
"Die With a Smile" becomes the fastest song ever to reach one billion Spotify streams

THE WEEKND

The Weeknd is one of Spotify's most-streamed artists. His honest songwriting has created countless hits.

GOING VIRAL

The Weeknd wrote music while working at a clothing store. He posted songs on YouTube. They quickly went viral. He made his first mixtape in 2011.

BILLBOARD'S GREATEST

The Weeknd's 2015 album *Beauty Behind the Madness* won two Grammys. *Billboard* named 2019's "Blinding Lights" the greatest Hot 100 song in history. In 2025, his After Hours Til Dawn tour became the best-selling tour in R & B history.

TIMELINE

2010
The Weeknd's songs begin going viral

2011
The Weeknd's debut mixtape *House of Balloons* is released

2016
***Beauty Behind the Madness* earns two Grammys**

A DARKER SOUND

The Weeknd has earned seven Hot 100 number ones. He has brought an alternative sound to R & B.

HIT RELEASES

Beauty Behind the Madness **(2015)**

Starboy **(2016)**

Dawn FM **(2022)**

Hurry Up Tomorrow **(2025)**

Birthday:
February 16, 1990

Hometown:
Toronto, Canada

Types of Music:
alternative R & B, pop R & B

First Hit Song:
"Love Me Harder" featuring Ariana Grande (2014)

2021
Billboard **names "Blinding Lights" the greatest song in Hot 100 history**

2025
The After Hours Til Dawn tour becomes the best-selling tour in R & B history

THE FUTURE OF R & B

Today's producers often use Digital Audio Workstations. They can edit vocals and create beats on the same device. They produce classic sounds with fewer instruments. Trap and electronic beats are increasingly used in R & B. These blur the line between genres.

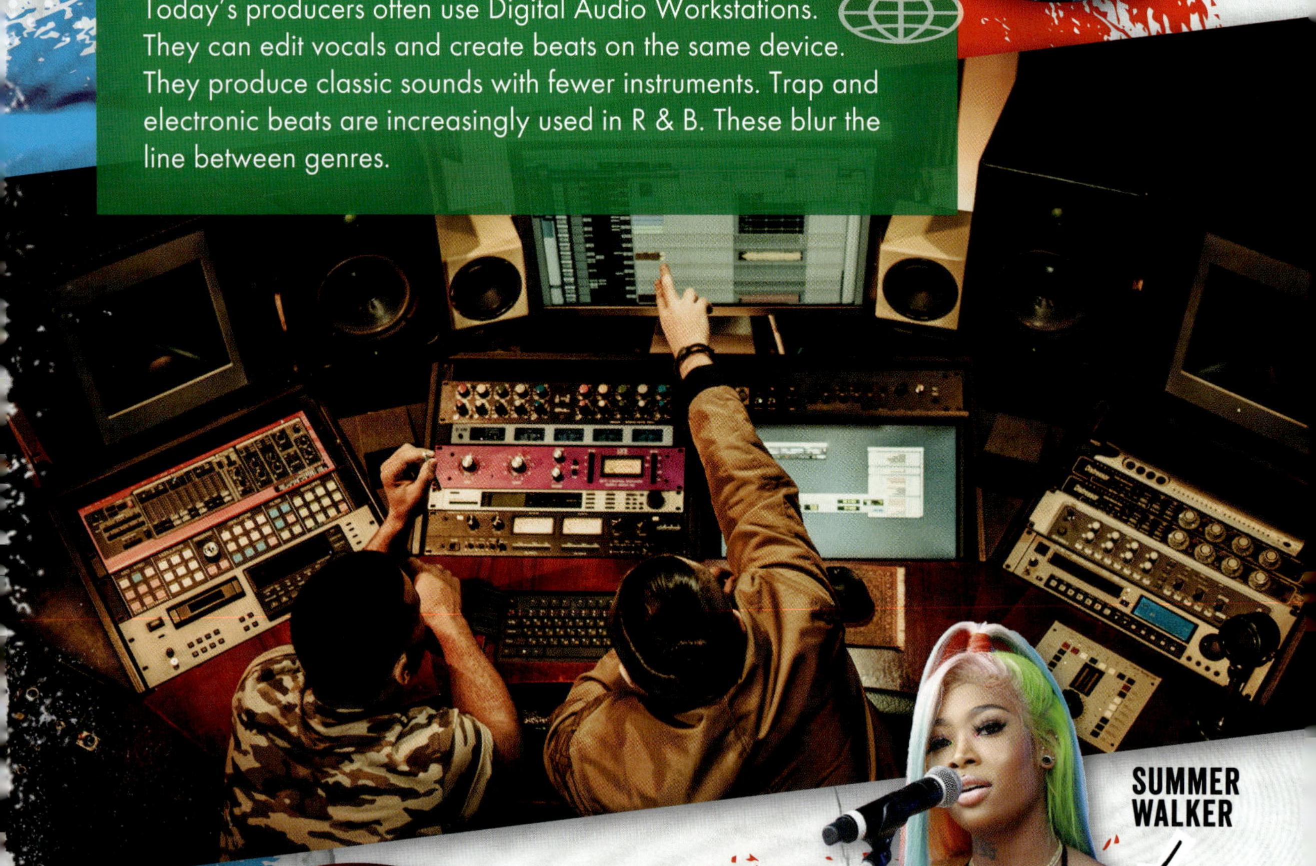

SUMMER WALKER

SZA and Summer Walker top modern R & B charts. Tyla and Tems blend the genre with African beats. Rosalía and Kali Uchis bring Latin sounds to R & B. Bryson Tiller and 6LACK have popularized Trap & B. R & B has a rich history. It continues to grow while staying true to its soulful roots!

GLOSSARY

advocated—spoke out and supported a cause

alternative—related to something different and typically outside of the mainstream

anthem—a song that is used as a symbol of power or importance by a group

ballads—slow and emotional songs that often tell a story about love

choruses—catchy, repetitive parts of songs that illustrate the song's main message

civil rights—people's rights to freedom and equality

collaborated—worked with others to create something

debut—first appearance

Digital Audio Workstations—computer programs that allow vocals to be recorded and beats to be made using the same device

doo-wop—a style of R & B and rock and roll where a lead singer sings with harmonizing backup singers, often without instruments

generation—a group of people who were born around the same time

genre—a category for a type of music

gospel—a type of religious music made famous in Black churches

harmonized—having two or more voices singing different notes at the same time

improvised—created something unplanned on the spot

inspired—gave someone an idea about what to do or create

melodies—series of lyrics and sounds that are arranged with a rhythm

mixtape—a collection of songs, usually released for free by an artist

nomination—the processes of being chosen as a candidate for an award

octaves—groupings of eight musical notes that can be sung or played

Oscar—a yearly award presented for achievements in film; Oscars are also called Academy Awards.

percussion—instruments that make sounds when struck or shaken

rhythm—a repeated pattern of movement or sound

samples—lyrics or beats taken from existing songs that are reworked and edited into new music

subgenres—smaller, more specific types of music within a genre

swing—a type of jazz music with danceable beats often performed by large bands

synthesizers—electronic musical instruments that can create sounds and change existing sounds

viral—popular from being shared quickly

visual albums—albums released as films or with each song having an individual music video

WRITE ABOUT IT!

- Which artist do you think has had the biggest impact on R & B? **Why?**
- What are some of your favorite R & B songs? **Why do you like them?**
- How do you think R & B will continue to **change** in the future?

ALSO CHECK OUT

INDEX

The images in this book are reproduced through the courtesy of: Anton Vierietin, front cover (hero); zamrznutitonovi, front cover (saxophonist); suteishi, front cover (trombone); Perkus, front cover (drums); Raph_PH/ Wikimedia Commons, pp. 3 (Mariah Carey), 5 (middle), 11 (2025), 25 (top left), 32 (left), 33 (Mariah Carey 37 (left, right); Robert Hoetink, pp. 3 (Beyonce), 36 (Beyonce, bottom), 37 (Beyonce); Adam McCullough, pp. 3 (Usher), 5 (bottom), 34 (Usher), 35 (Usher); hurricanehank, p. 4 (top); Brian Friedman, pp. 4 (bottom), 34 (bottom), 40 (middle left); ph.FAB, p. 5 (top); Michael Ochs Archives/ Stringer/ Getty Images, pp. 5 (inset), 8 (right), 20 (middle), 23 (1959); londonexpat/ Wikimec Commons, p. 6 (inset top); Heinrich Klaffs/ Wikimedia Commons p. 6 (left); Greg Miles, p. 6 (right); Soul Train/ Contributor/ Getty Images, p. 7 (top); Pictorial Press Ltd/ Alamy Stock Photo, p. 7 (bottom); Dave Hogan/ Contributor/ Getty Images, p. 8 (left); Kathy Hutchins, pp. 8 (bottom), 10 (1959), 31 (bottom left), 35 (Billboard award), 43 (bottom); Jorge Mejía peralta/ Wikimedia Commons, p. 9 (top left); Kobby Dagan, p. 9 (top right); A. Jama p. 9 (bottom left); Christian Bertrand, pp. 9 (bottom right), 42 (left, bottom); Moog Music/ Norlin/ Wikimedia Commons, p. 10 (1964); Atlantic Records/ Wikimedia Commons, pp. 10 (1967), 20 (top); J. Edward Bailey/ Wikimedia Commons, p. 11 (1971); Anthony J. Davis, p. 11 (1980s); Featureflash Photo Agency, pp. 11 (1990), 29 (bottom), 31 (middle top), 33 (bottom), 35 (middle); RadulePerisic, p. 12 (top); Ben Houdijk, pp. 12 (bottom 13 (bottom), 18 (left), 18-19 (middle), 19 (top), 45 (Kali Uchis, Rosalia); badnews86dups, p. 13 (top); Zde/ Wikimedia Commons, p. 13 (middle); ZUMA Press, Inc./ Alamy Stock Photo, p. 14 (top); Gregg DeGuire/ Contributor/ Getty Images, p. 14 (bottom); ANGELA WEISS/ Contributor/ Getty Images, p. 15 (top left, bottom left); s_bukley, pp. 15 (top middle 27 (bottom), 38 (left), 40 (top left); Bernd Schwabe/ Wikimedia Commons, pp. 15 (top right), 23 (grammy), 25 (grammy), 27 (grammy), 31 (grammy), 32 (grammy), 36 (grammy), 37 (grammy), 41 (grammy), 42 (grammy); Theo Wargo/ Staff/ Get Images, p. 15 (bottom right); United States Department of Defens Wikimedia Commons, p. 16 (top); United Archives/ Contributor/ Getty Images, p. 16 (bottom); Nikola Spasenoski, p. 17 (left); Grindstone Media Group, p. 17 (right); lev radin, pp. 19 (bottom 28 (middle right); The White House/ Wikimedia Commons, p. 20 (middle top); Kevin Ruck, p. 20 (bottom); Jarc12030/ Wikimedia Commons, p. 21 (top right); Anthony Barboza/ Contributor/ Get Images, p. 21 (middle); MCT/ Contributor/ Getty Images, p. 21 (bottom); 3DMI, pp. 21 (Hall of Fame), 31 (Hall of Fame); Denni MacDonald, p. 21 (Medal of Freedom); Gijsbert Hanekroot/ Contributor/ Getty Images, p. 22 (top left); Jim Britt/ Wikimedia Commons, p. 22 (top right); Jim Britt/ Contributor/ Getty Images, pp. 22 (bottom left), 23 (bottom); Sergey Novikov, p. 22 (bottom right); Los Angeles Times/ Wikimedia Commons, p. 23 (top); Rob Bogaerts/ Anefo/ Wikimedia Commons, p. 24 (top left); Eric Ko for Anefo/ Wikimedia Commons, pp. 24 (top right), 25 (top righ Jack de Nijs for Anefo/ Wikimedia Commons, p. 24 (middle); Jgphotographydetroit, p. 24 (bottom); SNEHIT PHOTO, p. 25 (Detroit); The_Supremes_1967/ Wikimedia Commons, p. 25 (bottom); UCLA digital library/ Wikimedia Commons, p. 2 (left); Michael Putland/ Contributor/ Getty Images, p. 26 (right); Aaron Rapoport/ Contributor/ Getty Images, p. 26 (bottom); Jacob, p. 26 (Saginaw); Tamla/ Wikimedia Commons, p. 27 (to Everett Collection, pp. 28 (top), 29 (middle right), 32 (top), 34 (top right), 39 (top); CBS Television/ Wikimedia Commons, p. 28 (middle left); Barry King/ Contributor/ Getty Images, p. 29 (top); KMazur/ Contributor/ Getty Images, p. 29 (middle) Matt Gush, p. 29 (Gary); Dirck Halstead/ Contributor/ Getty Images, p. 30 (left); Jim Smeal/ Contributor/ Getty Images, p. 30 (right); CBS Photo Archive/ Contributor/ Getty Images, p. 30 (bottom); Leonid Andronov, p. 30 (Newark); Jeppe Gustafsson, p. 31 (The Bodyguard); McSleepy, p. 32 (right); AITFFan1/ Wikimedia Commons, p. 33 (Huntington); taniavolobueva, p. 34 (top left); Debby Wong, pp. 34 (middle top), 39 (middle); Jeff Kravitz/ Contributor/ Getty Images, p. 34 (middle bottom); SeanPavonePhoto, p. 34 (Dallas); Tinseltown, p. 36 (top); DFree, pp. 37 (bottom), 43 (top); Kovacs, p. 37 (Houston); A.RICARDO, pp. 38-39; landmarkmedia, p. 38 (bottom); Mario Hagen, p. 38 (St. Michael); Sorbis, p. 39 (botto Jaguar PS, p. 40 (top right); Kevin Mazur/ Contributor/ Getty Images, p. 40 (middle); MNStudio, p. 40 (Honolulu); Fabio Dier p. 40 (bottom); John Shearer/ Contributor/ Getty Images, p. 41 (main right); Anthony Wright, p. 41 (middle); Bill Raymond, pp. 4 (right), 43 (middle); ronniechua, p. 43 (Toronto); Delmiro Junior, p. 44 (Tyla); Nejron Photo, p. 44 (studio); Hunter Crenian, p. 44 (SZA); Michael A Walker Jr, p. 44 (Summer Walker); Franklin Sheard Jr, p. 45 (Tems); Taylor Hill/ Contributor/ Getty Images, p. 45 (Bryson Tiller); Prince Williams/ Contributor/ Getty Image p. 45 (6LACK).